Designer
Cards & Tags
with
Dena

Designer
Cards & Tags
with

Dena

A LARK/CHAPELLE BOOK

A Division of Sterling Publishing Co., Inc.
New York

A Lark/Chapelle Book

Chapelle, Ltd., Inc.
P.O. Box 9255, Ogden, UT 84409
(801) 621-2777 • (801) 621-2788 Fax
e-mail: chapelle@chapelleltd.com
Web site: www.chapelleltd.com

10 9 8 7 6 5 4 3 2 1

First Edition
Published by Lark Books, A Division of
Sterling Publishing Co., Inc.
387 Park Avenue South, New York, N.Y. 10016

Text © 2006, Dena Fishbein
Photography © 2006, Lark Books

Distributed in Canada by Sterling Publishing,
c/o Canadian Manda Group, 165 Dufferin Street
Toronto, Ontario, Canada M6K 3H6

Distributed in the United Kingdom by GMC Distribution Services,

Castle Place, 166 High Street, Lewes, East Sussex, England BN7 1XU

Distributed in Australia by Capricorn Link (Australia) Pty Ltd.,

P.O. Box 704, Windsor, NSW 2756 Australia

Library of Congress Cataloging-in-Publication Data

Fishbein, Dena.
Designer cards and tags with Dena / Dena Fishbein. -- 1st ed.
    p. cm.
"A Lark/Chapelle book."
Includes index.
ISBN 1-57990-989-2 (hardcover)
1. Greeting cards. I. Title.
TT872.F57 2006
745.594'1--dc22
                              2006023940

ISBN 13: 978-1-57990-989-5
ISBN 10: 1-57990-989-2

For information about custom editions, special sales, premium and
corporate purchases, please contact Sterling Special Sales Department
at 800-805-5489 or specialsales@sterlingpub.com.

Table of Contents

How I Got Started

Once upon a time, a young college student ventured into a greeting card company, with a big bag full of drawings in each of her hands. She had never thought of herself as an artist, but with her mother's encouragement, she had decided to try her hand at designing greeting cards. Would this be the day she got her big break?

Well, no and yes. The art director who met with her did not take one look at her work and declare her the next rising star. But he was very kind and spent an entire hour talking with her about what he looked for when selecting designs. He urged her to make each element on a greeting card the absolute best she could, explaining that because a greeting card offers such a limited space, it's especially important that even background details receive the same care and attention as the focal point, and that all the elements work together for the overall design.

As you probably have guessed, I was that girl, and the experience was my first, tentative step into what has turned out to be a long, happy adventure in designing greeting cards. A few years after meeting with the art director, I combined some technical drawing experience I had gained in college with an experimental, playful approach to painting; developed my own style; and started licensing my designs to a greeting card manufacturer. Since then I've made my living designing images and patterns and developing products, including greeting cards for Sunrise Greetings, a division of Hallmark. Over the years I've even been fortunate enough to win a number of Louie Awards. (These are like Academy Awards for greeting card designers.)

Along the way, I have also made and received countless handmade cards. You might think that there's a big difference between designing a commercial card and creating a handmade card for one special person. In truth, handmade cards do allow a designer to use materials and add personal touches that aren't practical for mass-produced items. Yet whether a card is designed for one special person or for many, the advice the art director gave me back when I was getting started is as sound as ever, and I share it with you now: pay attention to the details. Be as thoughtful in your choice of background and accents as you are with the main image. Use the best materials you can afford for the project, and the sharpest skills you possess. Not only will the recipients of your cards appreciate the extra care, but with every new project, you'll also find yourself growing as a designer and an artist.

I save every handmade card I get. The fact that someone took the time to create something just for me is as special as the message written inside.

The audience, message, and mood of your card should guide your design decisions. For this baby shower card, I wanted to evoke the same feeling we get when we look at a baby, so I chose happy colors and an image that has what I think of as the "Aw Factor."

Designer Secrets

The goal of this book is to offer you a wide range of projects, along with tips that will not only help you replicate these projects, but will also help you learn to think like a designer. That way, whatever materials you use and whatever look you want to achieve, you'll know how to make well-informed design choices. While I explain my approach to specific cards throughout the book, this chapter describes some of my general principles and techniques—my "designer secrets." Please keep in mind that every designer develops a unique approach based on her or his personal tastes, preferred techniques, and favorite materials. There's no one right answer—the most important thing is to find what works for you.

In this chapter, I explain how to create great handmade cards:

- Create a Connection
- Be (a Little) Practical
- Trust Your Eye
- Learn Timesaving Tricks
- Be Inventive with Everyday Items
- Color Copy Messages
- Master Basic Techniques

Designer Secret I: Create a Connection

A well-designed card makes an emotional connection with the recipient. After all, the purpose of any card is to help reinforce our relationships. Whether making or buying a card, you must answer a few questions: Who is it for? What message do you want to send? What mood do you want to evoke? To make an emotional connection with the recipient, your card's design must reflect your answers to these questions.

When I receive an assignment from a commercial client, I'm given information about the target recipient's age and gender, and the occasion for the card: "Boy Age 3 Birthday" or "Grandmother Easter." This information narrows my design choices considerably. A choo-choo train in primary colors is about as likely to appeal to a grandma as a big bouquet of pastel-colored flowers is to catch the eye of the average three-year-old boy. Obviously, when I create a card for a friend or family member, I have an even more specific audience in mind. But whether your card is intended to appeal to a broad category of people or a specific person, considering what images and colors the recipients are likely to find appealing will help you connect with them.

Our Family

When you're making cards for specific people, you can make the emotional connection even stronger by choosing their favorite colors and images that refer to their interests. You might even use a personal photo, as this card does.

It's also important to think about the message you want to send. Sometimes, the message is implied by the simple fact that you've given someone a card—the message is that you care. At other times, the message is made even clearer through text (called "editorial" in the card design business) and image. The mood your card evokes can also be seen as part of the message. Do you want the recipient to smile? Feel reassured? Say "Aw"? Remember she's a cool, sassy chick? Your answers to these questions can help you decide if you want a style that's sweet or sophisticated, bold or subtle, whimsical or traditional—or a combination.

Designer Secret 2: Be (a Little) Practical

A major difference between commercial and handmade card designs is that handmade cards offer the designer a lot more freedom. Commercial card designs have to accommodate the requirements of mass production and store sales. Bits of vintage jewelry and layers of fabric—easily incorporated into a handmade card—are too difficult to find and cost too much for mass production. There's also the issue of what's called "rack appeal." Typical store racks reveal only the top third or so of a card, thus a salable design needs to catch the buyer's eye with that small area.

A handmade card goes straight from creator to recipient, and the personal connection virtually guarantees that it will be read carefully. You can make your design as elaborate as you wish and place your elements wherever they look best.

When designing cards for Sunrise Greetings, I help consumers recognize the message at a glance by placing the main text in the top third of the cover.

Yet even with this freedom, there are other practical considerations to take into account. For instance, if you're creating multiple cards, such as wedding invitations, you may want to select a design that won't require special postage, as oversized or oddly shaped cards do. You should also consider your budget and the time you have to spend on making a card. After all, if you need to knock off a dozen thank-you cards in an hour, you'll want to select a simple design (or one that accommodates shortcuts).

Designer Secret 3: Trust Your Eye

Part of the reward for creating a handmade card is the personal satisfaction of seeing your design come together. Of course you want the card to please the recipient, but it can also be an expression of yourself. Using a design that reflects your taste and interests is like sharing a part of yourself with the recipient.

Many people are hesitant to take chances and trust that their instincts will lead them to beautiful designs. Yet I firmly believe that everyone can learn to create cards that they love. In addition to reading books like this one and looking closely at what elements contribute to the cards you most enjoy, give yourself plenty of practice. Start by gathering materials you like to see combined, then audition each material, placing it here and there with the others, adding more materials, and taking some away until you like what you see. You can also learn a lot by trying to create your own versions of your favorite designs, whether you copy them exactly or substitute alternative materials. For this reason, I've supplied tips about the construction and composition of my designs throughout this book.

With few exceptions, the projects in this book were designed in sets. They will, I hope, help you to see the endless possibilities for different combinations of similar elements. It's also helpful to have coordinated items for certain occasions, as when you need complementary invitations and thank-you cards, or are giving a card and a present with a gift tag.

With handmade cards, the designer has more freedom to place elements because the card is not likely to be sold from a rack. I particularly love to layer elements—glitter, buttons, beads, etc. You can go over the top with the design because you don't have to worry about how practical it is to mass produce.

Designer Secret 4: Learn Timesaving Tricks

If you want cardmaking to be a regular part of your life, or if you plan to make multiple cards at once (as with invitations), you can streamline your project time in a number of ways. The most important trick is to collect materials ahead of time. This step is, hands down, the most time-consuming, and if you have to go hunting for materials for every new project, chances are you won't make that many cards. Every time I pop into a used bookstore or wander through a flea market, I'm on the lookout for items that catch my eye. By adding a little to my collection every so often, I don't have to run out to the store when I want to make something.

It's also important to gather what you need before you sit down to make the card. Getting up to fetch scissors, then a bit of ribbon, then glitter glue can add a lot of time to a project. Worse, with all these interruptions, you may lose your

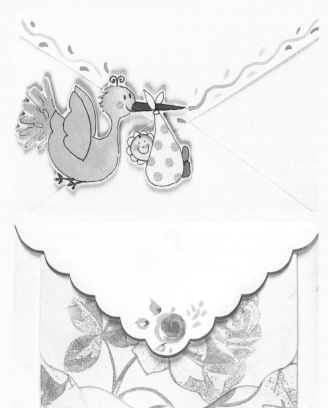

My favorite timesaver is to use purchased envelopes for my handmade cards. Sometimes I'll decorate the outsides, but I prefer to focus on the cards than on things that will get battered in the mail, ripped open, and then tossed in the recycling bin.

In this book, I use a number of terms to explain my designs:

BALANCE—Balance refers to the relationship between different elements. A balanced design encourages the reader to notice the card as a whole, not just an element or two, while also supporting the importance of the focal point.

MAIN IMAGE—In this book, I use this term to refer to the dominant image on a card, such as a cake or a vintage lady. It may be color copied and added to the card, or collaged out of papers and/or other materials.

FOCAL POINT—The focal point is the part of the card that attracts and holds the viewer's eye and is usually the main image, if there is one. Be sure your focal point reflects the message and/or mood you wish to create.

BASE CARD—Most cards begin with a plain, sturdy foundation that is scored and folded if necessary, then decorated. To create my base cards, I usually mount pretty papers on illustration board.

BACKGROUND—The background is the first decorative layer applied to the base card. Choose background elements that enhance, rather than distract from, the focal point.

COLOR PALETTE—Often shortened to just "palette," this term refers to the range of colors on a card. The color palette is a very important part of creating mood and overall style. Limiting your palette can help you achieve a more unified design.

TEXTURE—Texture (smooth or rough, for example) can refer to the feel of actual materials, or to the illusion of texture that can be created by color copying materials such as satin or burlap.

DIMENSION—Anything that calls attention to the card as a three-dimensional object is said to "create dimension." Using foam dots to lift an element higher than its background is one of my favorite ways to create dimension; adding windows and frames, which produce recesses, is another.

UNITY—A design is unified when all the elements are tied together visually and conceptually, and make the viewer aware of the whole card rather than just a section of it.

CARD—This general term covers all the card types, including flat cards, framed flat cards, tags, tri-fold cards, and the standard type of card that opens from the bottom or side like a book.

FLAT CARD—A flat card doesn't open. For flat cards, you can make your message part of the design or write it on the back, as you would on a postcard.

FRAMED FLAT CARD—This type of card has a frame adhered to the front; the frame adds a little extra dimension. I often use these cards for invitations and announcements.

TAG—A tag is a relatively small, one-sided card. It can be any shape you please, but if it's a rectangle with the top corners clipped off (like an old-fashioned shipping tag), it's said to be "tag-shaped."

TRI-FOLD CARD—This card is created from a long rectangle of cardstock that has been folded to create three panels.

creative focus and compromise the quality of the card, your pleasure in making it, or both. For cardmakers who don't have a dedicated craft space (and that's most people!), I recommend tossing what you need for a project into a box or a basket. That way, you can tote your materials to the kitchen table, the living room, or wherever you'll be crafting, and keep them together if you have to move them aside quickly for dinner, visitors, or the million-and-one other things life brings your way.

Craft and scrapbook supply stores abound with special tools and materials to help time-crunched cardmakers. You can make gorgeous cards without using paper trimmers, scoring boards, hole punches, and premade elements such as bows, layered embellishments, stickers, and envelopes, but when you're in a hurry, they sure can come in handy. Printing or color copying images directly onto heavy cardstock or using heavyweight scrapbook papers can save you the step of backing lightweight papers with illustration board.

Designer Secret 5: Be Inventive with Everyday Items

With the variety and beauty of scrapbook papers we can use in our cards, it might be easy to overlook another great source for paper patterns and images: the world around us. Anything is fair game. From leftover gift wrap and paper drink parasols to buttons from old clothes, great cardmaking materials are everywhere. One of the easiest ways to distinguish your projects from anyone else's is to create your own papers from unusual items in your environment. For example, I color copied sections of old wallpaper and antique textiles to create many of the background papers used for the projects in this book. A number of embellishments come from my personal collection of vintage ephemera—again, color copied so I can use the images over and over. I love the color copier, but other folks prefer to scan their materials into computers and print them on color printers.

Flea markets, thrift shops, and used bookstores can be great sources of vintage ephemera, such as postcards, newspaper clippings, and the like. There are also fabulous collections of images available at bookstores—usually such "clip art" is offered for free use, provided you don't try to sell it. (For instance, I couldn't use such an image in one of my commercial designs.) At the end of this book, there's a section called Angel Art (see page 130). There you'll find a number of my own illustrations and patterns that you are free to copy and use for your personal projects.

Designer Secret 6: Color Copy Messages

Because invitations and announcements typically go out to many people, it's essential to save time when creating the text for these types of cards. Rather than create each card from scratch, I suggest trying one of two methods.

The first method is to scan the background paper into a computer and use a desktop publishing program to overwrite your message on the patterned background. Then, you can either print out one color copy and reproduce it on a color copier, or you can print multiples right from your color printer. The pros tend to use the first method, so if you don't have the equipment or expertise, and if the occasion is formal, it might be worth getting help. But for many of us, the second method works just fine and is much simpler: just apply alphabet stickers, stamp letters, or print directly onto the background paper and use a color copier to reproduce as many invitation messages as you need.

Color copying and printing can get expensive. One way to cut costs is to create a master that repeats the invitation message to fill a standard 8½ by 11-inch page. (Just be sure to account for the border around the text when laying out the master.) This will provide you with multiple messages on each color copy you make. Then you can use a paper trimmer to cut apart the messages quickly and cleanly.

By repeating the invitation text multiple times on a master page, you can save money on copying costs.

Designer Secret 7: Master the Basics

Just as every designer has a unique style, most cardmakers find different ways to achieve the same ends. For instance, where I might use glue or spray adhesive to mount paper onto illustration board, another cardmaker might prefer to use double-sided tape. The techniques described here are the ones I used to create the projects in this book; feel free to use other techniques if you're more comfortable with them.

Creating a Base Card

The base card is similar to a painter's canvas—it's what you build your design on. Whether I'm making a tag, flat card, framed flat card, tri-fold card, or standard card, I typically create a sturdy base by covering illustration board with a decorative paper, using spray adhesive or polyvinyl acetate (PVA) glue (see Mounting Lightweight Papers, below). If you have a heavyweight scrapbook paper or decorative cardstock you want to use instead, then you can skip mounting it onto illustration board.

For standard and tri-fold cards, score the folds for cleaner edges. You can purchase a scoring board (it looks like a paper trimmer), but with practice, it's just as fast and much more economical to place a metal ruler along the fold line and run a craft knife very lightly along the ruler, taking care to cut through the top layer of the paper only. Then fold the card and run a bone folder along the fold.

To make a framed flat card, begin with two sturdy layers that are the same size and shape. Use a craft knife to cut a window into the top layer, then place the window over the bottom layer to determine the placement of images or text on the bottom layer. You can adhere the two layers together before or after decorating them; choose according to your design. Most of my framed flat cards are rectangular, though it's also fun to explore alternatives, such as the oval-shaped frame of the Easter Egg Card (see page 68). As a shortcut, you can also use small, precut mats, often found in scrapbook stores and in the frame sections of craft shops.

Finishing a Card's Interior

Since I usually fill a card with a personal note or other text, I don't often feel the need to embellish the interior. If you feel a card needs an extra touch, adhere a coordinating paper, and, if you wish, cut and add a paper frame to your note, or add a small image. Just take care not to add so much to the interior that the card won't close.

Mounting Lightweight Papers

I'm a big fan of mounting thinner papers onto heavier ones. It makes them easier to work with, and adds dimension to the card and durability to embellishments. My base of choice is illustration board—it's fairly inexpensive, sturdy, and easy to work with. (See page 16 for more on illustration board.)

To mount lightweight paper onto illustration board, I usually use a foam brush to spread a thin, even layer of PVA glue across the back of the paper, press it to the illustration board, and smooth it from the center to the edges with my fingers or a brayer. If glue might spill out from the edges of the paper, place a layer of waxed paper between the project and the brayer to protect the brayer. To mount large pieces, such as a background paper, I may use spray adhesive instead (working in a well-ventilated area, of course!).

Creating Dimension

As you'll see from the projects in this book, I like to add interest to handmade cards by playing with the heights and depths of different elements. For instance, to bring an image into the foreground, I may apply it to the card by using foam dots. To give an element the importance of a special setting, I may surround it with a layered frame or cut a window around it. Embellishments such as lace, pompom trim, and textured ribbon offer other great ways to build dimension into a design, as do free-hanging miniature tags and interactive features, such as cards tucked into pockets.

When adding dimensional elements, try to use the appropriate adhesive. Fine-tipped glue (see Tools and Materials, right) can be critical in giving small elements a nice, clean look. Sturdy double-sided tape is great for adhering ribbons and other materials that may discolor if wet.

Adding Glitter

Glitter. We learned to love it in preschool, but many of us shy away from it as adults, haunted by memories of globs of sparkle and bald patches of glue. The two keys to glittering like a grown-up are to control your adhesive and to choose your glitter carefully.

For delicately glittered borders and accents, you'll need fine-tipped glue. Keep a piece of scrap paper handy to catch that initial blob of glue, and, if you have any doubt about the steadiness of your hand, practice drawing lines with glue before you apply it to your card. For the Cupcake Card project

BONE FOLDER—Use this smooth-edged, blunt tool to make clean, sharp creases in heavy papers.

CRAFT KNIFE—Similar to a utility knife, a craft knife has a razor-blade-style cutting edge mounted on a penlike handle. I use mine mainly for cutting out windows. Lay your project on scrap cardboard or a cutting mat to protect surfaces and the blade.

FABRIC RIBBONS AND TRIMS—You don't have to pay top dollar for your ribbons or for trims such as rickrack, but do pay attention to quality. Better ribbons give handmade cards a noticeably richer look and feel. Stock up at craft store sales or shop online for great values. In my opinion, it's much better to use just a touch of top-quality ribbon than a whole lot of ribbon that's second-rate.

FINE-TIPPED GLUE—Many brands of craft glue for paper come in bottles with narrow tips, but if you can't find a type you like with a tip that's narrow enough, buy an empty, fine-tipped applicator bottle at a fine-arts supply store and fill it with your favorite liquid craft glue.

FOAM DOTS—These are circles or squares of foam with adhesive on both sides; they allow you to give elements extra dimension. I like the time-saving aspect of using precut dots, but you can also cut pieces of foam tape for the same effect.

ILLUSTRATION BOARD—Heavier than standard cardstock but lighter than cardboard, illustration board is a great backing for lightweight papers. I use it to give strength to base cards, images, frames, and other elements. If you can't find it at your craft store, try a fine arts store, use heavy cardstock, or, in a pinch, use the cardboard from a cereal box. (In general, I avoid the last option because the acid content in the cardboard may affect the project's longevity.)

LIQUID CRAFT GLUE—There are many brands of general-purpose craft glue. Read the label to make sure that the glue is suitable for use with paper, and try a few types until you find a kind you like. PVA glue works well.

METAL RULER—A metal ruler isn't just for measuring and drawing straight lines; it can also serve as a guide for your craft knife when you're scoring or cutting out windows.

PAPER PUNCHES—A regular small-circle punch does the trick for most situations. Occasionally, I'll use special paper punches to cut out large squares, rectangles, ovals, or tag shapes. If you're having trouble getting clean shapes with a large punch, place the punch on the floor and compress it with your foot. Save leftover shapes and outlines for other projects.

PREMADE FLOWERS—Steer clear of ordinary silk flowers; they tend to make a project look cheap. Instead, select flowers made of other fabrics or paper. I particularly like the appearance of millinery flowers, available in packets or straight off old hats that I find at tag sales.

SPECIALTY SCISSORS—Craft stores offer an amazing variety of scissors for making just about any shape of cut imaginable. After straight edges, the two essential lines I need are scalloped and zigzag. I also like to have a pair of craft scissors with very sharp, very short blades for cutting out small and detailed shapes.

(see page 34), I wrote a line of cursive letter e's in order to get fairly uniform swirls of glitter. For an all-over glitter effect, apply a coat of spray adhesive, sprinkle on the glitter, let the glue dry, then shake off the excess.

The glitter you use will also have a huge impact on how sophisticated your results look. For the most part, avoid the kind of glitter that kids use. Use fine crystal glitter instead—it's more subtle. I usually use clear crystal glitter, as it lets the colors of the project beneath it come through, but sometimes I prefer the effect of using a color. When I want an authentic vintage look, I use a small-flake glitter called "German mirror flake." This type of glitter is made from mirrors, and, as it conceals whatever's beneath it, should be used with special care.

The one trick from grade-school glittering that I do use is to glue-and-glitter in stages whenever I'm using multiple colors on a single project. For example, if I'm using gold glitter on one element and blue glitter on another, I'll place the glue for the gold only, sprinkle on that color, let it set, then shake it off before repeating the process for the blue glitter areas.

Aging Paper

With a little help, new materials can take on vintage character. The method I use most often is to lightly tap a sponge loaded with brown ink along the edges of a project or embellishment. Some craft stores sell miniature sponge pads, about the size of an eraser, that are specially made for this purpose. I also like to use brown florist's spray to achieve an aged look. Practice on scrap paper first to master the touch.

Tools and Materials

You don't need a lot of fancy materials to create great cards. If you have a few scrapbook papers, adhesives that are suitable for your materials, a pair of scissors, and a pencil, you're good to go. Still, to make the kind of cards I like, I've found that some materials are indispensable. Please see the section on the left for a list of my favorites.

Happy Birthdays

There are a million ways to say "Happy Birthday."
The best way, in my opinion, is the one that matches
your personal expression to the interests and tastes of
the person being celebrated. Creating a handmade card
enables you to do exactly that. The designs in this
chapter cover a range of styles, but as you look through
them, keep in mind that there are countless ways to
adapt these projects in order to make them the perfect
"Happy Birthdays" for the people in your life.

Nifty Poodles

The poodle is more than a beautiful dog (and I'm not saying that just because I have one!). It's also an icon of the 1950s girly-girl. For this set of projects, to recall the fun, flirty mood of that era, I paired a photocopied image from a vintage greeting card with a fifties-style color palette of pink, black, and aqua. Using fine-tipped glue, I collaged the same paper hat, pompom nose, and rhinestone collar onto each dog, but I varied the backgrounds to create a distinct look for each project.

Black Poodle Card

To make this project particularly suitable for invitations and thank-you cards, I saved time by using a premade bow for the present and a heavyweight scrapbook paper that doubles as the card base and background. From a design point of view, note how a background with a large floral pattern and a darker pink than the one used in the Gray Poodle Card calls for a stronger image, such as a black poodle that is taller than the base card. Black trim along the bottom balances and unifies the whole look.

Poodle Tag

Extending an element past its background gives a design a more dynamic feel; the present in this tag, and the hat and bow of the Black Poodle Card are good examples. A black-and-white harlequin border along the bottom contrasts with the polka-dotted background and the vertical stripes on the present, bringing still more energy to this tag. To keep the design from becoming too busy, I used a single touch of aqua at the focal point, and I unified the overall design with a black bow at the top of the tag.

Gray Poodle Card

A pinstriped background and polka-dotted border give structure and energy to the background of this design, while the soft pink color and subtle black geometrics keep it in a supporting role. To create the present and hat, I color copied a scrap of wallpaper that I found at a flea market; it adds an authentic retro touch. By playing with the settings on the copy machine, I lightened the poodle from black to gray, making the area that includes the dog's black nose and the red rose on the present the focal point of the card.

Paper Princess Dresses

Make a princess of any age feel like the royalty she is by presenting her with a fantasy gown for her birthday. To make sure a cute image is appropriate for grown-up tastes, choose a sophisticated palette, such as aqua, brown, and pink. If you want a more convincing illusion, keep miniature elements to scale, as in the Aqua Dress Tag and Pink Dress Card. To heighten the make-believe magic, float the main image against a relatively oversized background, as in the Birthday Princess Card.

Aqua Dress Tag

This dress tag is a good example of keeping elements to scale. With the exception of the eyelets, the details maintain the proportions you might see on a real dress, right down to the pattern on the paper used for the gown. Even the largest element—the paper flower—stays within the realm of possibility. (The Aqua Dress pattern is available on page 132.)

Pink Dress Card

To make this flat card, I mounted paper onto illustration board and cut out the shape of the dress. Then I pleated a bit of tulle, glued it at the waist of the dress, and covered the gathers with a wide ribbon. To finish, I used fine-tipped craft glue to add dressmaker-style details—the flower, pearl buttons, and pompom trim—and attached the tag to a miniature hanger. (The Pink Dress pattern is available on page 132.)

Birthday Princess Card

Sensible brown plays dress-up with pink polka dots, making the perfect background for a gown any princess would love. (The Dress and Crown images are available on page 132.) To create a card like this one, with a flap on the right, determine the finished size of the card and make a base that is twice as wide plus whatever width you want the flap to be. Score and fold the base twice—once for the left edge and once for the flap.

Baby's First Birthday

When designing for young children, it's good to choose simple designs that make it easy for their inexperienced eyes to recognize the focal point. Cheery baby animals hold universal appeal for little ones, and with gentle background colors and straightforward layouts, the main image on each of these projects stands out.

Elephant Tag

To add a punch of color without distracting from the main image, adhere a narrow strip of striped paper to the bottom of a tag cut from polka-dotted paper. Notice how it highlights the scalloped bottom edge of the polka-dotted paper and gives some definition to the tag. (The Elephant image is available on page 133.)

Bear Card

To keep the focal point of this card strong but not overpowering, use a background paper that contains more subdued shades of the colors found in the main image. Also note how the rickrack along the bottom is a slightly paler green than the green of the cupcake wrapper, while the real birthday candle (tucked into a slit cut in the cupcake) provides the most intense color in the whole design. (The Bear-and-Cupcake image is available on page 132.)

Giraffe Card

If you want to use a bright background paper, such as the striped base of this card, you can prevent the main image from getting lost by backing it with paler paper. A light green ribbon is the crowning touch—to add it, punch two holes in the dotted paper, thread the ribbon through them, then adhere the paper to the base card. (The Giraffe image is available on page 133.)

To create high-energy designs that don't get too busy, keep the design principle of unity in mind when selecting your materials. Each card in this set uses contrasting patterns and bright colors for the backgrounds, but because key colors are repeated throughout, the effect is cheerful, not chaotic.

FIRE

Brandon's turning 3!
join us in the celebration
Saturday, August 12th
at 1:00 pm

Train Card

In this card, different background papers repeat the yellow in the main image—the train. Blue rickrack at the left border and red pompom trim at the right edge repeat other key colors, reinforcing the design's overall unity. Other ways in which I prevented the complex background of this card from overwhelming the focal point included using a relatively subtle paper for the main background, helping the focal point to pop by adhering it with foam tape, and presenting the message in a white cloud that contrasts with the bright colors around it. (The Train image is available on page 133.)

Fire Truck Invitation

For this framed flat card, I cut a window into plaid scrapbook paper and glued it to the blue-and-yellow dotted invitation message. To finish, I used foam tape to add the fire truck and fine-tipped glue to add the stars. I liked how the red truck blended in with the plaid background, but you can place it against a contrasting background if you prefer. The beauty of creating your own designer cards is that you get to tailor them to your taste! (The Fire Truck image is available on page 133.)

Car and Truck Tag

Strips of scrapbook paper make a colorful landscape for cars and trucks to race through. Rickrack in different widths and hues provides a fun, wavy border between the lanes. As with the other designs in this set, the main idea is to create unity, despite the range of colors and patterns, by repeating colors across the page. (The Car and Truck images are available on page 133.)]

thank you

Please join
Madeline Grace
for a tea party
to celebrate her
5th birthday
Sunday, May 14th
at 2:00 pm

Carriage Bears

One of the things I like best about designing sets of projects is that I don't have to choose just one way to present a favorite image. Instead, I can play with the different effects made possible by changing patterns, embellishments, and layouts. While you're free to duplicate any of these designs for your handmade cards, I encourage you to experiment with the many different ways in which you can present a favorite image of your own. (The Carriage Bear images are available on page 134.)

Carriage Bear Tag

While an image mounted to a simple base with a foam dot can make a charming tag by itself, sometimes just one more element brings it all together, such as a slip of vellum attached with a safety pin.

Carriage Bear Thank-You Card

This design works equally well for a flat card or a standard folded card. To create it, color copy the main image, mount it on illustration board, cut it out, and adhere it to the top of a card cut from polka-dotted paper. Punch two holes in the center of the carriage, thread a grosgrain ribbon through them, and adhere a metal-edged tag to the space between the holes. I like the personal touch of a handwritten "Thank You" on the tag, but if you prefer, use tiny stamps or stickers to create your message.

Carriage Bear Card

With a pretty hat on the bear and a flower print for the carriage, the main image is transformed in a way that invites new possibilities. A contrasting background could make this design busy, but thanks to a plaid paler than the main image and to the solid-colored borders along the top and bottom of the card, the eye is still carried to the focal point.

Carriage Bear Invitation

The gingham paper used for this framed flat card had a white border around the center, some flowers, and a preprinted butterfly. You can easily duplicate the effect by layering cutouts or stickers onto scrapbook paper then color copying this master for multiple invitations.

Victorian Animals

Using vintage images doesn't mean a design has to be stuffy. For these cards, I placed Victorian animal images in a dignified setting of classic plaid—then I added contemporary polka dots and topped each one with a party hat. To me, it's the contrast between their solemn expressions and these playful touches that makes the results funny in a stylish, British-comedy sort of way.

Let's Party

Victorian Bulldog Invitation

Clearly, this bulldog means business—from the red pompom on his hat to the charm saying "Let's Party" dangling from his neck. Use a patterned paper for the interior of the card, score and fold it, then adhere plaid scrapbook paper to its front outer panel. Adhere rickrack to the inside bottom edge of the card. Mount a bulldog image on illustration board or cardstock, add the hat, and adhere it to the back of the card. Write the party information on the card's interior and tie the charm to the dog's neck to finish.

Victorian Terrier Birthday Card

When making a card for a real animal lover, it's worth adding all the extra touches found in this design. After cutting an oval window into plaid paper and bordering it with red rickrack, I glued crimped white paper to the inside of the window frame. Then I used foam dots to mount the dog image on the interior of the card, aligning it with the window. But the real *coup d'grace* is, I feel, the dog's crocheted trim collar, tastefully accented with a bit of rickrack and a blue rhinestone charm, as befits such a high-class canine.

Victorian Tabby-Cat Tag

A solemn puss gets dressed up in an Elizabethan ruff made from rhinestone trim, and a "plume" made from a stiff, striped ribbon. In case there's any doubt that this tag is meant to be a little bit silly, the center is a scalloped circle of playful paper.

Cupcake Trio

Combining elegant papers with a fun theme can make a design more
interesting. These projects use a regal, embossed scrapbook paper and a
ladylike pastel palette, not with something expected, such as a beautiful
vintage flower, but with a more playful birthday icon—the humble cupcake.
For a more realistic effect, the cupcakes are "wrapped" in paper that has
been crimped and trimmed along the top with pinking shears. To make the
images even more unusual, each one is embellished with a piece of real
costume jewelry, such as a pin that the recipient might wear.
(The icing on the cupcake, so to speak.)

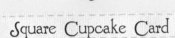

Square Cupcake Card

The technique used to create this card is the same as that used for the Victorian Terrier Birthday Card (see page 33). The materials I used include text from an old book, an earring found at a tag sale, and a gold foil paper called "Dresden" to edge the window. The finishing touch is seam-binding ribbon tied around the fold of the card. Please keep in mind, however, that you don't need these exact materials to produce the same effect—aim for similar colors and textures, and your recipients will enjoy them just as much.

Cupcake Card

To me, the fact that some of the jewels on this card's vintage pin are missing only adds to its charm. After all, you'd never find an authentic piece of costume jewelry on a commercial card! And because the pin isn't shiny and new and perfect, it gives the other materials greater depth and character. (For great old jewelry finds, look for packages of mismatched and broken pieces at flea markets.)

Cupcake Tag

Some people shy away from mixing metallics, such as the silver-toned earring pinned to this tag and the gold-based glitter swirls on the cupcake's icing. I find that if you keep the metallic tones at the same level of intensity and they suit the overall design, mixing golds, silvers, coppers, and so on can add richness without clashing; but, as always, this depends on the overall design—trust your eye.

Soft Florals

If you need a pretty, feminine card in a hurry,
you can't go wrong with the designs in this set.
First, color copy the Cake or Bouquet image (see
pages 134–135), create the card base, and use
foam dots to apply the image to the card. Punch
two holes side-by-side, thread a length of 3"-wide
tulle (found in the craft-store bridal section)
through the holes, tie a bow, and *voila!*
It doesn't get much easier than this.

Soft Floral Bouquet Card

If you can't send a luscious bouquet of real roses for someone's birthday, try this card. For added interest, finish the inside with a light-weight scrapbook paper in a pattern that contrasts with the cover—tiny polka dots or lovely miniature rosebuds. Or choose a different color entirely, such as a subtle cream.

Soft Floral Bouquet Tag

This tag uses the same cake image as the Soft Floral Cake Card, which I reduced on the color copier. A sweet paper daisy hot-glued to the center of the bow gives a little bit of substance to the cloudlike effect of the tulle and pastel paper.

Soft Floral Cake Card

A background paper of soft, impressionistic flowers makes this card ultrafeminine—perfect for the true romantic on your card-giving list. Glue a gold-toned ribbon along the base of the cake if you'd like to give the image a stronger presence.

Cutie-Pie Birthday

Great vintage images can be found in old books and ephemera that you pick up at secondhand bookshops, thrift stores, and tag sales. But if you have trouble finding just the right thing, look into a recently printed collection of images. For these projects, I used images from *The Adventures of Dolly Dingle*, a book of reproduction paper dolls (Dover, 1985). If the style of the little girl looks familiar, it's because she was created by Grace G. Drayton, the same illustrator who did the famous Campbell's Soup Kids campaign.

Cutie-Pie Tag

Even a simple tag can be enriched through dimensional elements. After collaging the doll image to striped, heavyweight scrapbook paper, add a miniature card that opens, a pink paper hat that extends beyond the top of the card, and a touch of soft chenille yarn.

Cutie-Pie Card

A skirt made from a genuine embroidered handkerchief is the sort of dimensional detail that makes a handmade card different from a commercial one. When working with unique materials, you may want to start with the unusual item and base your palette on it, unless you have a large collection to select from.

Cutie-Pie Cake Card

This design is perfect when you want to say "Happy Birthday" to someone who has a real sweet tooth. Start with pink rosebud scrapbook paper, and collage on a retro paper doll and an aqua ruffle to put under a big, chocolate-frosted cake (adhered with a foam dot for dimension). Top the doll with a hat trimmed with aqua chenille yarn and finish by tying yarn around the fold in the card. When adhering larger items such as the doll and the cake, be sure to spread a thin layer of glue completely across the item and use a brayer to smooth the paper evenly.

Welcome, New Baby

Each new baby reinvents the world. Each one
calls for a celebration. When I design cards
for expectant parents and baby showers,
I find myself with a smile on my face,
thinking of all the joy a new life brings.

It's a girl!

Our precious baby arrived on
June 21, 2005
at 4:13 pm
he weighed 8 pounds, 2 ounces
and measured 21 inches long

Amy Olivia

42

Fairy Godbunnies

As you may have noticed, I like to combine classic choices with unexpected touches. It's fun to do, and the results appeal to a wide range of people. For this set of projects, I gave the traditional color for baby girls a bit of a twist with touches of yellow and green, and created a bunny illustration with wings and a crown (available on page 134).

44

Fairy Godbunny Card

If you love the fabulous layered embellishments offered in craft stores, but can't find exactly the right one for your project, why not create your own? Start by adhering together an image such as the Fairy Godbunny, a circle of paper lace, a folded ribbon, and a scalloped-edged circle of scrapbook paper. Using foam dots for added dimension, attach the image to the project and position a brad through the top fold of the ribbon.

Fairy Godbunny Announcement

A framed flat card can be as simple or as fancy as you like. A scalloped border with black penned details defines the outer edges of the frame, while green ribbon draws the eye in to the birth announcement. Touches of crystal glitter on the fairy bunny take only a moment to add, but give it the kind of detail that makes a handmade card special.

Fairy Godbunny Tag

A layer of lavender vellum gives this tag extra personality. The bunny image, mounted on a circle cut from a paper doily, covers the dots of glue that I used to adhere the vellum in place.

It's a girl!

r precious baby arrived

June 21, 2005

at 4:13 pm

Vintage Lambs

A few elements and a simple layout can add up to a classic, understated design when you pay close attention to placement and details. Because the main image of an antique pull-toy used for this set of projects could be overwhelmed easily, I chose to support it with subtle white-and-blue paper and minimal embellishments. To soften the gap between a vintage image and new papers, I rubbed brown ink along the edges of each card.

New Baby

Vintage Lamb Window Card

Window cards allow their recipients to enjoy a main image twice—first when they slip the cards from their envelopes, and again when they open the cards. To enhance the Victorian feel of the pull-toy image, I used a deckle-edged square punch to create the window on this card. Because the lamb image and the white buckle are aligned, I positioned the base card paper with its pattern off-center for a more dynamic background.

Vintage Lamb Card

Have as much fun discovering new ways to play with your embellishments as you do with the other elements of your designs. A gold tag picked up the warm hue of the lamb's platform, but it looked too plain on its own. A crimped strip of vellum was the right solution: its horizontal place-ment balances the flap and introduces another texture, yet the soft color and translucent quality of the vellum keep this element in the back-ground. With the support of such a subtle embellishment, simply placing the lamb image so that it extended below the edge of the flap was enough to give the image the emphasis it needed.

Vintage Lamb Tag

Whether designing a tag for yourself or for others, consider where a handwritten message would go and how it might affect the final look. For instance, when planning this design, I imagined I'd write a very brief message across the bottom. Since I wanted the impact of a large tag but wanted to avoid leaving dead space, I folded a white ribbon and layered it under the main image.

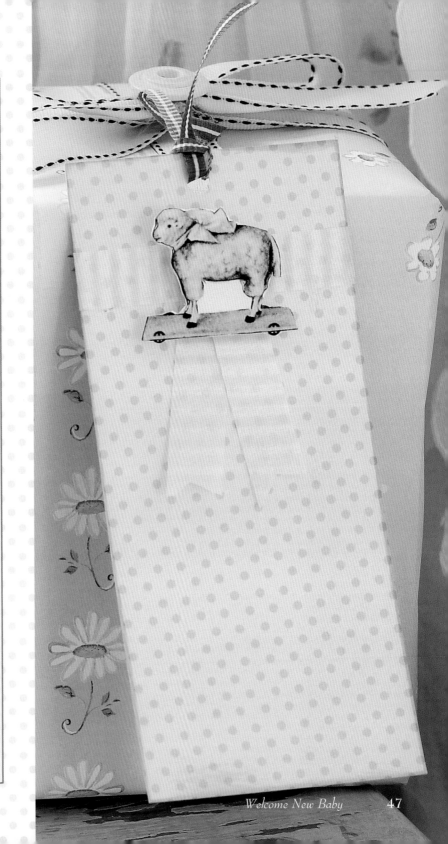

Laura and David
are happy to announce
the arrival of their precious baby boy
on October 5th
at 2:56 am,
weighing 8lbs, 5oz

Ian Michael

Contemporary Lamb Set

I wanted to create a set of designs that had the same simple elegance as the Vintage Lamb projects, but with a more contemporary feel. To do this, I kept my embellishments minimal and my layouts clean and formal, but I went with a more modern color palette and illustration. (The Contemporary Lamb image is available on page 134).

Contemporary Lamb Announcement

By combining a whimsical image with a clean, symmetrical layout, this framed flat card strikes a balance between the fun of welcoming a new child to the world and the classic look of a formal announcement. To create this card, follow the techniques for a framed flat card and for color copying invitation messages (see pages 14-15). Add a striped grosgrain ribbon that picks up colors from the main image, gingham-covered brads, and the main image mounted on foam dots. A tag placed directly below the image completes the presentation.

Contemporary Lamb Tag

What I like about this design is that it's a fast, easy project that has a lot of impact, thanks to the dimensional presentation of the main image. Simply use foam dots to mount an image onto a rectangular tag, punch a hole through the top of the image, and tie on a ribbon and paper flower.

Contemporary Lamb Card

The fewer elements you use, the more important it is to place each one strategically. For this project, a subtle, blue-patterned background paper extends beyond the center of the card. This could throw the design out of balance if it weren't for the more intense effect of the pink dotted paper used on the right. The ribbon covering the seam between the papers strengthens the balance with stronger shades of key colors, and pulls the viewer's eye to the main image. To reinforce the focal point even further, I used foam tape to give it dimension and framed the image with punched paper flowers. (Look closely—a rhinestone at the end of the lamb's pull-string is the sort of detail that makes a handmade card even richer.)

Victorian Baby

Some of my favorite papers for handmade cards don't start off as papers at all. Color copies of vintage wallpaper give me authentic colors and patterns for "period pieces," such as these versions of Victorian cards. But even when I'm going for an authentic look, I can't resist adding a modern twist—in this case, the dimensional touches not found on standard commercial cards of any era.

a Baby Shower

To: From:

Victorian Cradle Tag

Though less elaborate than the Victorian Baby Card, this design still uses three levels of dimension: the cradle, which serves as both background and foreground, and the baby, which rests in the middle. A glitter border defines the edges of the tag to help it stand out against whatever package it's tied to.

Victorian Baby Shower Card

The rose wallpaper makes a great paper for images, too. After cutting out an umbrella shape and mounting it on the card, I added a pipe-cleaner handle, a plain brad at the top, and glitter-glue spokes for the umbrella top. A die-cut tag tied to the handle is a final dimensional touch, but even with all these details, the card can be made quickly enough to be used for invitations or thank-you cards.

Victorian Cradle Card

The key to this design is dimensionality. First, I created the main image by cutting a slit into a cradle image, tucking a baby image inside, and mounting it with foam dots. To give the image more presence, I positioned it against a trio of red roses that was part of the background paper. The contrasting color of the roses adds drama, and the triangular shape, which mirrors the swags of the cradle like a luxurious second curtain, gives the image more depth. Lace at the foot of the cradle extends the visual plane further. Even the glitter glue on the edge of the cradle and the chenille yarn around the fold of the card serve to enhance the card's dimensionality.

Ducklings

For a refreshing alternative to the traditional pink or blue often used for baby cards, try a palette of pastels that includes aqua, green, and yellow. Incorporating playful touches such as feathers or a fleece diaper also helps take a design in a new direction. (The Duckling image is available on page 135.)

Duckling Card

To give a relatively small image stronger presence on a large card, use foam dots to mount it onto layers of circles punched from coordinating papers. Extend the image further by adhering a delicate white plume between the layers of paper. Another way to help the image seem more prominent is to split the background; for instance, this card has gingham paper along the top and plaid paper on the bottom.

Square Duckling Card

The small tag tucked into the fleece diaper on this card can carry a baby shower invitation, birth announcement, thank-you, or personal message to an expecting parent. To create this project, cut a square card from pastel plaid scrapbook paper and trim the right edge with scalloped shears. Cut a triangle from white fleece, fold in the corners, and glue the diaper to the center of the card at an angle. For the tag, cut a small square from gingham scrapbook paper, adhere the duckling image to the top, and tuck the tag into the fleece diaper.

Duckling Tag

Sometimes a combination of textures is all you need to give a design interest. The soft feather, ribbon tie, and scalloped border of the base tag make this simple project rich with detail.

Baby Boy in the Moon

Some people have a hard time designing for boy babies. To avoid making a feminine-looking card, they reach for primary colors and images of cars and trucks—not the best choices for welcoming a tender new baby. When in doubt, I suggest combining gentle colors with geometrics, such as the dots, harlequins, and stars used for this set of projects.

Welcome to the World!
Jacob Ryan
May 9, 2005
at 6:36pm

Kevin, Andrea and proud big sister Hannah

Our Sweet Baby

Celebrate

Baby Boy in the Moon Card

A top-opening card can be a refreshing alternative to traditional card structures. To create this card, make a base with a flap large enough to stay closed. You can also make this design with a flat card base, using foam dots to mount a strip of polka-dotted paper along the top.

Baby Boy in the Moon Announcement

If you're computer-savvy, you can create and color print a flat card like this one, complete with border and announcement, then apply your image and sentiment by using foam dots. If you're not, you can replicate this design by layering a frame onto a base with the invitation message printed on it to create a framed flat card (see Creating a Base Card on page 15).

Baby Boy in the Moon Tag

When you need a tag with room for more than a "To" and "From" message, a long, rectangular tag can be just the ticket. Because the image is tied to the top and can dangle free, even the background behind it can provide space for a personal note.

Baby Bears

Texture plays an important role in hand-made cards. Soft touches of fleece and chenille yarn make these projects inviting to the touch. If the recipient is expecting a boy, or you'd like a gender-neutral card, simply use different colors for the back-ground and embellishments.

Baby Bear Card

Even grown-ups can't resist a cute, interactive feature, such as a cut-out bear that can be tucked into or pulled out of a soft fleece blanket. To create the blanket, cut a square from fleece, fold the side corners in and the bottom corner up, pin them in place, and glue the blanket to the card. (The Bear with Heart and Umbrella Carriage images are available on page 135.)

Baby Bear Invitation

To create this cheery card, score and fold pink polka-dotted scrapbook paper, line it with pink-and-green striped paper, and use scal-loped scissors to trim the pink paper about an inch from the front right edge. Then, use foam dots to apply the carriage image to the card, glue the "Baby Shower" umbrella in place, and tuck the bear into a carriage embellished with a bit of chenille yarn.

Baby Bear Tag

A quick tag doesn't have to be dull. After cutting a tag shape from heavyweight scrap-book paper, glue on a color copy of the bear image and a rectangle of fleece trimmed with pinking shears. Finish the tag with a ribbon tied through a hole at the top, and a punched paper flower with a rhinestone center at the bottom.

Cute as a Button Ginghams

Sweet little gingham shirts and pockets are cute yet unusual for baby shower cards. By layering papers with the same pattern but different colors, you can create a rich background, as in the Gingham Shirt Card and the Gingham Pocket Tag. A contrasting paper offers different possibilities and may even invite a play on words, as with the Cute as a Button Card.

cute as a button

Cute as a Button Card

Be inventive when creating your own versions of the designs pictured here. If you can't find button-patterned paper for this card, stamp, draw, or glue buttons on plain yellow cardstock and color copy the image. Likewise, you can shape a small hanger from wire or a paper clip rather than purchasing a ready-made hanger at a craft store. The differences in the small touches will make your cards unique. (The Small Shirt pattern is available on page 136.)

Gingham Shirt Card

A fleece collar, real buttons, and rickrack all build dimension into this design and support the focal point—the bunny peering out from the yellow pocket. When layering same-patterned papers, find ways to define the elements. For instance, the green base card peeking out from behind the yellow gingham background serves as a subtle border for the entire card. Hand-drawn "stitches" around the yellow pocket pick up the touches of black from the bunny's face, giving weight and definition to the focal point. (The Bunny image and Shirt and Pocket patterns are available on pages 135-136.)

Gingham Pocket Tag

To assemble this tag, punch four holes along the top of the pocket, thread cord through them (leave a large loop on the front), and apply the bunny image while also positioning the cord loop to hang between the bunny's paws. To finish, cut a rectangle from yellow gingham paper and cut notches at each end. Place it over the cord loop and adhere it in place with foam dots.

Holidays

Holidays are the perfect times to reach out to friends and family with handmade cards. Whether the occasion is sacred or secular, play with your materials and discover ways to fuse traditional images and ideas with fresh approaches.

Vintage Valentines

Who says a valentine has to have a giant red heart? With backgrounds of antique wallpaper in faded yellow, these designs defy the clichés of the holiday while still conveying messages of affection. The authentic vintage image— found on an old greeting card at a flea market—is enhanced by a glittery red heart.

Vintage Valentine Card

The style of this card is what I call "vintage-with-a-twist." All the elements are items that might have been available many years ago, yet the color combination and layout are more contemporary. To create this card, use foam dots to mount a color copy of a vintage lady onto a base card, and add a pink Dresden foil border along the left edge. Glue on a pleated paper skirt and a doily overskirt then add a glittery heart to finish.

Vintage Love Card

The wallpaper I color copied for the bottom half of this card had a wonderful border edged in pink—perfect for layering with another wallpaper sample for the base of this card. The head and shoulders of my vintage greeting card girl peek up from behind the card, holding a heart that reflects the color of the letters used for "Love."

Vintage Valentine Tag

A charming vintage image and paper lace doily grace the top and bottom of this tag. Details such as this one, along with the pink glitter on the heart and the Dresden foil along the seam between the tag and the doily border, take a little more time, but can make a nice tag an extraordinary one.

Hearts-and-Flowers Valentines

Heart shapes and pretty flowers—for some, no Valentine's Day is complete without them. Make these classic images new by using a palette that includes blues, greens, and yellows, and by including unusual materials, such as color copies of authentic vintage handkerchiefs.

Hearts-and-Flowers Card

The handkerchief that I color copied for my background paper had a red flower border that worked nicely for the right and bottom edges of this card. For the main image, I used illustration board to back a color copy of another handkerchief, punched out a scalloped heart, and surrounded it with a strip of black-dotted tulle before mounting it with foam dots to the card. The "ribbon" tied in a bow at the fold of the card is really another strip of sheer fabric—a trick that opens more possibilities to a designer than relying on ribbon alone.

Hearts-and-Flowers Tag

For an unusual Valentine's Day gift tag, back a heart cut from a yellow floral print with a black-and-white gathered tulle trim. I color copied a handkerchief for this project, but a scarf, tablecloth, or other textile with an appealing print would serve just as well.

Hearts-and-Flowers Tri-Fold Card

Make a grand impression with a card that offers heart after heart to your valentine. First, use spray adhesive to mount polka-dotted paper onto illustration board, then cut a large rectangle and trim the edges with pinking shears. Score and fold the rectangle into three equal panels and apply a layered heart to each one. The base of each heart shown here was cut from color copies of antique handkerchiefs, bordered with translucent fabric trims, and embellished with millinery flowers. To finish, I wrote "I," "Love," and "You" on glittery heart tags and used foam dots to apply each tag to a large heart.

Easter Parade

Cards for springtime holidays call for bright colors and cheerful patterns that reflect the optimism of the season. While brainstorming designs for this set of Easter-themed projects, I came up with country ginghams, which seemed like a natural match for a duck motif. For a subtler look, you can use a pastel palette or substitute a simple floral for the striped paper. The Duck image—color copied at different sizes for each project—is available on page 136.

Easter Egg Card

The traditional Easter eggs that hold beautiful scenes inspired the design of this framed flat card. It's built from two layers adhered together: an acetate-backed oval frame trimmed with rickrack, and a blue floral background, to which color copies of a duck image have been applied using foam dots.

Easter Tag

To create this project, mount striped paper onto illustration board, punch a large oval, and glue pink rickrack to the back of the oval, making sure the rickrack shows from the front of the tag. Using a foam dot, apply the duck image to the tag, punch a hole at the top, and thread a pink gingham ribbon through the hole.

Easter Duck Card

The gingham pattern of this card's background gives it energy, while the pale pink hue offsets the brighter colors of the main image. A strip of paper along the fold and a feather on the top are the small touches that make a handmade card appear well planned and polished.

Mother's Day Tea Set

For me, brainstorming images for handmade cards often begins with a feeling. Thinking of my mother evokes warm comfort—like a nice pot of tea. The fact that sharing tea with Mom is a tradition in my family makes the images of teapots and a teacup even more appropriate. As a bonus, these images work well as cutouts; it's easy and fun to create their shapes from pretty papers. (The Teacup and Teapot patterns are available on page 137.)

Teacup Card

Pockets are interactive elements that make a design fun. Here, the teacup is adhered to the card base along the sides and bottom only so that a heart-shaped note can be tucked inside—perhaps with a bag of Mom's favorite tea. When choosing papers for this project, keep in mind that geometrics such as polka dots can make florals livelier and more interesting. Don't worry about matching colors as long as they play off each other in ways you find appealing.

Teapot Card

Flowers punched from the same paper as the background tie together the main image of a teapot, the paper border along the left edge, and the floral background. A bit of rickrack, adhered to the inside of the cover's right edge, subtly draws out the warm yellow touches in the floral paper.

Teapot Tag

A teapot-shaped tag is the perfect accompaniment for a box of Mom's favorite tea. To create the tag, mount floral paper onto illustration board, cut out a teapot, and embellish it as desired.

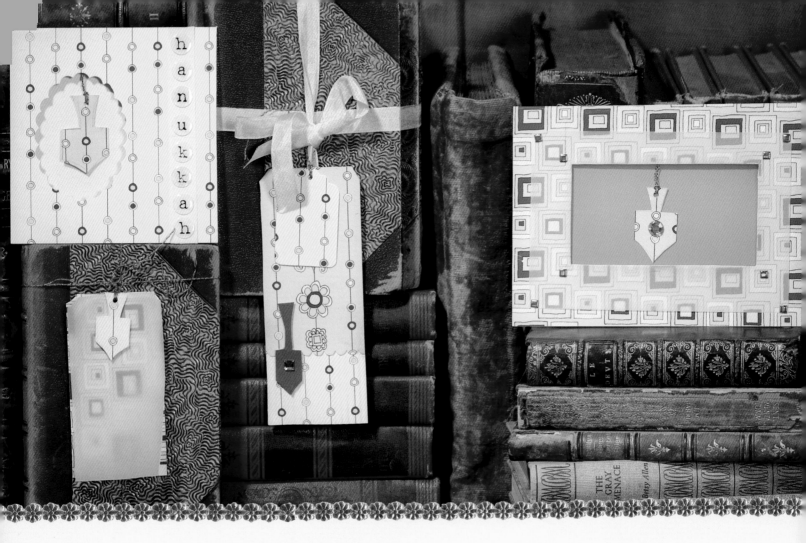

Hanukkah Greetings

Giving tradition a little twist is often simply a matter of playing with color. The colors of Hanukkah—blue and white—become aqua and cream, with touches of brown to give these designs a hipper, edgier look. A little rhinestone here, some crystal glitter there, and the image of a dreidel keep the mood appropriately festive.
(The Dreidel patterns are available on page 137.)

(The Dreidel patterns are available on page 137.)

Hanukkah Card

This card offers an easy yet high-impact way to wish loved ones the happiness of the season. A dreidel-shaped cutout hangs from a scalloped window punched in the cover. To hang the dreidel, tie cord through a hole punched in the top of the image, then tape the other end of the cord to the back of the window.

Small Dreidel Tag

Vellum can make a contemporary print seem a little more formal. A tiny dreidel, tied to the top of the tag, is a playful touch.

Large Dreidel Tag

The layered effect of this project makes it a tag—and then some. To create the base of the tag, cut a large rectangle from aqua paper and trim the top corners at an angle. Then trim the bottom with scalloped scissors and adhere a rectangle of cream paper to the back of the scalloped edge (with the pattern facing the front) to create a border at the bottom of the tag. Punch or cut a small tag from cream paper. Punch holes in the tops of the large and small tags, and tie them together with a ribbon. Cut out a dreidel shape from brown paper, use foam dots to apply it to the tag, and glue a blue rhinestone to its center.

Dreidel Card

Although this card opens from the bottom, its cover is made using the technique for making a framed flat card (see page 15), with the addition of a vellum overlay on the front. To create the overlay, cut a rectangle of vellum that is larger than the window but smaller than the frame. Adhere it to the front of the card, using double-sided tape or a special vellum adhesive found at craft stores.

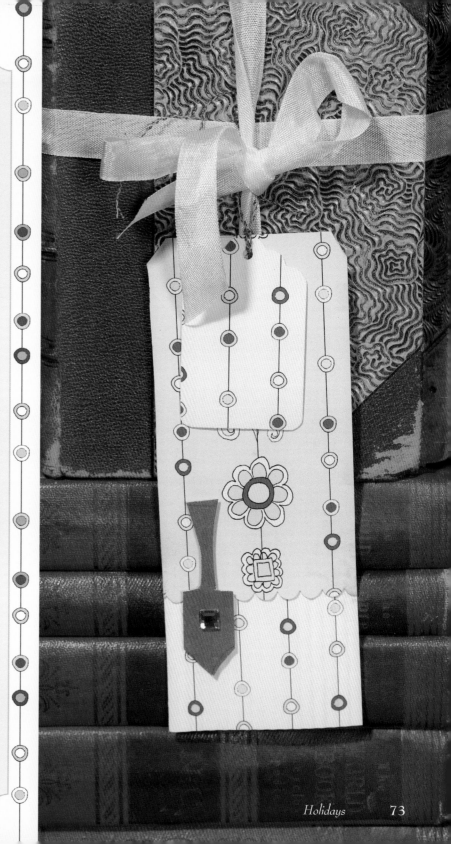

Christmas Fun

As with the Hanukkah cards, these designs pair traditional images with a slightly unusual palette. Here, red becomes pink, and, for two of the projects, green becomes a wintry mint. The result is a set of holiday cards that conveys the feeling of the season while standing apart from the crowd on the mantel, the way a set of handmade cards should.

Winter Scene Card

The vintage image of children with a snowman changes the tone of the pink-and-mint color scheme to something more retro than contemporary. To build on the nostalgic feel, I added a "necklace" made from a scrapbook tag, with a twisted cord "chain" and a red cord along the top of the pink border. To create the scene, punch a scalloped hole in the card cover and adhere the images to the back of the window so that they peer out.

Christmas Stocking Card

A pink stocking trimmed with fleece can hold an invitation to your open house, a gift card, or just your wishes for the holidays, written on a miniature card. To create this card, first make a flat card base by layering mint patterned paper on top of a slightly larger rectangle of pink patterned paper. (I used scrapbook papers, but gift wrap can work well, too.) Cut a stocking shape (the Stocking pattern is available on page 138) and adhere it to the card along the side and bottom edges only. Embellish the shape with a glitter-glue outline, a strip of fleece, and a pink button.

Christmas Stocking Tag

The stocking that serves as a pocket on the Christmas Stocking Card can be a beautiful tag as well. Use heavyweight paper or mount lightweight paper onto illustration board, top with a strip of fleece, and apply a small tag to the center for your message.

Silly Santas

The Santa image used for these projects has dangling arms and legs that make it a little interactive and a whole lot of fun. With a slight alteration to the waistband and different background papers, the same image can be used for a greeting card, invitation, or gift tag. Just color copy the pieces, tape string to the backs of the mittens and boots, then tape the loose ends of the strings to the shoulders and legs of the body. (The Basic Santa image is available on page 138.)

Jolly Santa Card

Although you can easily use this Santa against a variety of patterns, a deep red paper with subtle stripes and dots creates a rich background that won't overwhelm the image's simple style. Edging the body with glitter, applying the main image with foam dots, and using a contrasting color for the belt are other touches that help keep the main image prominent.

Santa Tag

Because this design is super-simple to make, it's a perfect touch on gifts for neighbors, coworkers, and other groups. Color copy the pieces, cut them out, tape them together with string, and punch a hole for a ribbon in the top of the hat. If you'd like to go a step further, you can hide the tape by finishing the back of the body, the mittens, and the boots with coordinating paper.

Santa Party Invitation

To add a little more polish to this simple card, round the corners of the base. Because saving time is especially important during the holidays, you may want to invest in a round-corner punch rather than relying on scissors and a steady hand.

Everyday Occasions

Everyday occasions include personal holidays such as anniversaries and any other times that might call for expressions of gratitude, wishes for improved health, or reminders that life is full of reasons to smile. The designs in this chapter cover a range of occasions— I hope they inspire you to find many ways to make every day a cause for celebration.

Love and Thanks

The most common everyday reasons for
sending cards are to express love and
gratitude. Keep the messages light and
cheery, and the patterns and images
whimsical and contemporary.
These projects are fast and easy—
exactly what you need
when you're suddenly inspired to
reach out to a friend.

I LOVE YOU

I Love You Card

Sometimes you've just got to say it—or someone just needs to hear it. A flat card made from brightly colored paper is a great way to say "I Love You." For this design, layer a color copy of the Heart Mice image (available on page 138) onto polka-dotted paper, set a brad in each corner of the image, and adhere a paper flower above. Then punch circles out of green paper, stamp on the letters of your message, and adhere the circle to the card. To finish, glue pompom trim to the back bottom edge of the card, making sure the pompoms remain visible from the front.

Mouse Tag

Pretty up an everyday present with a tag cut from polka-dotted paper, and embellish it with a floral border, pompom trim, and a color copied image of one cheery little mouse (from the Flower Mice image, available on page 138).

Thank-You Card

Because it's essential to express thanks promptly, I designed this card to take only minutes to make. To create the base, score and fold patchwork-patterned cardstock. Then mount a color copy of the Flower Mice image onto green paper and use foam dots to apply it to the base. Cut out an orange banner, adhere it to the bottom of the green "frame," and spell "Thank You" with alphabet stickers. As a final touch, wrap a ribbon around the fold and tie a bow. If you have time, glue a rhinestone to the center of the mouse's flower—it's a nice extra touch.

Happy Anniversary

As I've already mentioned, one of the best ways to find unusual papers is to create your own. For this card and tag, I color copied a vintage, crepe-paper tablecloth that I found at a flea market, choosing sections I thought would give me particularly beautiful images. To enhance the vintage feel while keeping the design streamlined, I chose crimped paper for the borders rather than lace, and outlined the images with a variety of colored glitter.

Anniversary Card

Vellum is a material that adds instant elegance to a project, but it can be tricky to work with. To save time (and potential headaches), I purchased preglittered vellum for this card and the Butterfly Tag. To enhance the flowers and leaves on the base card, I applied glitter outlines by using a fine-tipped applicator to draw glue lines around the flowers, sprinkling on a pink glitter, shaking off the excess, and repeating the process to add green glitter to the leaves.

Butterfly Tag

Although I don't use German mirror flake often, there are times when it's the perfect type of glitter for a project. To create the heart embellishment on this tag's vellum overlay, cut a small heart from illustration board, cover it with a thin, even layer of craft glue, and sprinkle on the German mirror flake. Allow it to dry and shake the excess onto paper (save the excess for another project!). If there are any blank spots, apply more glitter.

Get Well

Creating an emotional connection with a card's recipient is never more important than when you want to express sympathy and encouragement. A vintage greeting card gave me the image of a cute puppy snuggled in bed—just the sort of thing that would make me smile if I were under the weather. To make the image more current, I cut it out of its original setting and experimented with different colors and patterns to create backgrounds with a more contemporary feel.

Get Well Gingham Card

Although the colors and patterns of this card give it a lot of energy, careful choices unify its design. For instance, the red gingham background shows around all four sides of the bed, framing the space with a single pattern that reinforces the red bedspread. Because the canopy has as much white in it as red, it blends in with the gingham behind it just enough to work with, not against, the border. The striped paper behind the bed pulls in yellow from the puppy, and white from the pillow and sheets. A red miniature clothespin holds the message "Get Well Soon" to the top of the bed, which is mounted on the card with foam dots.

Get Well Pompom Card

The same art used for the Get Well Gingham Card gets a solid yellow background, red pompom trim, and a miniature card instead of a banner for the message. To create deeper dimension, stack foam dots when applying the image to the card base, as I did here.

Flower Fairies

A face from a bit of vintage ephemera launched this set of designs. At first, I thought I'd collage a body for it, using only all-natural materials, but because I wanted the cards to be durable, I chose instead to use velvet leaves, silk flowers, pipe-cleaner arms, and German mirror flake wings. (The hair, however, is real moss, so I did manage to slip in a woodland touch!) The backgrounds for the card and tag are color copies of antique wallpaper, but you could easily substitute green patterned scrapbook paper for the same effect.

Flower Fairy Card

The secret to this fairy's charm lies in taking a free-form approach as you layer the elements. Think in terms of creating just the suggestion of a fairy image rather than building a real fairy, and you may be more open to the spirit of inspiration and fun that drives this design.

Flower Fairy Tag

If you're aiming for an all-around vintage feel, try to incorporate textures that may have been common in the era you're evoking. Velvet leaves and ribbon, silk flower petals, and old-fashioned German mirror flake (rather than synthetic glitter) are authentic to the Victorian period reflected in the face.

Felt Miniatures

Tiny clothes paired with floral papers make these projects both pretty and playful. The thick, soft texture of the felt used for the clothes adds dimension and interest to the designs. As a bonus, the material won't unravel and can be embellished by using ordinary craft glue, so it's particularly easy to work with. (The patterns for these projects are available on page 140.)

Pink Felt Dress Card

The formal design on the background paper and the tailored style of the dress make this card a touch more sophisticated than most, which is particularly nice for a girl who feels all grown up. A border of coordinating paper on the left, with a pink flowered ribbon along the seam, is a subtle way to add detail to the background without distracting the eye from the focal point.

Green Felt Skirt-and-Blouse Tag

Once you've established a theme for a set of projects, it's easy to brainstorm more images. After creating a variety of dresses, I moved on to this little skirt and blouse. To make this design, create a long base tag from pretty paper and round the corners. Adhere a wire hanger at the top of the base tag then cut one felt piece for the top and one for the skirt, trim the bottom edge of each piece using scalloped scissors, and use foam dots to apply them to the tag over the hanger. Finish with a row of beads and a bit of trim.

Blue Felt Dress Card

As any fashion maven knows, the shape of a dress's skirt changes its personality entirely. With a bell-shaped skirt, this card's main image begs for the freedom to dance across a floral background.

Blue Felt Sweater Card

A wide main image such as the sweater on this card can work especially well with a square background that has strong horizontal elements. Tiny hangers like the one on this card are available in craft stores, but if you prefer, you can make your own using wire and a pair of needle-nosed pliers.

Tropical Fun

Finding everyday occasions to celebrate is a great way to look at life. Whether you're throwing a housewarming party or a backyard luau, saying thank you, or simply spreading some cheer, light colors and party glasses will remind your friends to stop and have a little fun.

Tropical Drinks Card

A row of fancy party drinks like the ones served at tropical resorts sets a lighthearted mood—perfect for a friend who needs a mental vacation. To create this card, I drew and cut out images of glasses and used foam dots to apply them to striped paper. I then cut a frame in the cover of my base card and placed the paper with the glasses on the interior of the frame.

Pink Drink Card

A subtle striped background plays up the pinks of this card's main image while orange trim along the bottom gives the design a shot of warmth. To make the drink image even more inviting, fill the bottom of the glass with dark pink glitter. (The Pink Drink image is available on page 140.)

Cocktail Glass Tag

If you need a fast, fun tag for a housewarming party, print or mount the Cocktail Glass image onto heavyweight paper, punch a hole in the top, and tie it to your gift with a bit of ribbon. (The Cocktail Glass image is available on page 140.)

Ribbon Images

Sometimes the inspiration for a set of projects comes not from a particular theme, but from a particular technique. I was playing around with grosgrain ribbons one day, wondering what images I could make with them, when I folded back the ends and discovered a number of possibilities. My favorites—a big, pink present and a pair of handbags— are featured here.

Grosgrain Present Tag

Layering a narrow pink ribbon with yellow dots over the wide pink-and-white ribbon gives this tag a more interesting focal point. The bow, which is tied and glued to the card separately, makes the image a present rather than just an interesting square.

Green Grosgrain Purse Card

To create a purse with a little dimension, I folded the ends of my ribbon around a bit of cotton fluff and adhered a rickrack trim "handle" before gluing it to the card base and adding fabric flowers. To reinforce the effect of the vertical lines of the purse's stripes and handle against the strong horizontal stripes of the background, I added a thin ribbon border along the left edge of the card.

Yellow Grosgrain Purse Card

Using the same technique as the one I used for the Green Grosgrain Purse Card, I created the main image for this card and mounted it onto a simple card base with gently rounded corners. The geometric background paper seemed to me a perfect fit for the sporty style of the purse, but if you want to create a different mood, try a floral background instead.

It's Been Too Long!

It's too easy to fall out of touch with good friends. Weeks—months—sometimes even years pile up before we know it. Rather than wait until your friendship is just a memory, make and send a handmade reminder of how much you value your connection.

I miss you

It's been toooooooo long

I Miss You Card

Sometimes the best way to break a long silence is with a little humor. A heartfelt "I Miss You" gets the message across, while the smile on the dachshund's face reminds your friend of the fun you have together. To create this card, color copy the Dog image (available on page 139), adhere it to a long rectangle of white cardstock, and score and fold the cardstock into three equal panels. This project is as easy as it gets!

Call Me Card

To create a playful reminder that you're only a phone call away, cut out the silhouette of an old-fashioned telephone, give it a gold glitter outline, and tape the ends of a chenille yarn curl to the back of the silhouette before adhering it to a striped card base. For the center of the dial, punch a scalloped circle and a smaller circle from contrasting papers. Adhere the larger circle to the center of the telephone, and use foam dots to apply the smaller circle to the larger one. Punch more small circles for the keys, apply them around the center of the dial, and spell "Call Me" with dimensional acrylic alphabet stickers. Add the final touch—a bit of green trim along the bottom—and you're ready to write a newsy note inside. (The Telephone pattern is available on page 139.)

Animal Parade

The next time the kids need a fun activity, pull out sturdy paper circles, googly eyes, felt or fleece scraps, pompoms, buttons, markers, a hole punch and glue—and watch the creativity fly!

Bear Tag

A teddy bear's signature round ears and good-natured grin make this a cheerful tag.

Kitty Cat Tag

Multi-toned scrapbook paper, triangular felt ears, and pipe cleaner whiskers transform the basic project into a cat.

Pig Tag

Experimenting with different materials in different colors led me to a pig with a button for a snout.

Puppy Tag

Young crafters will love the soft texture of the puppy's ears and nose.

Elephant Face Tag

Cutting shapes from felt for noses and ears will give you the flexibility to create just about anything.

Weddings

A wedding should be as unique as the two people getting married. Whether the recipients are the bride and groom or their guests, handmade invitations, thank-you cards, place cards, and gift tags reflect the profound, personal importance of the momentous day as nothing else can.

Traditional Wedding

The paper for these designs came from a piece of fabric that I found in my closet and color copied onto matte paper, but you could copy a piece of Grandmother's veil or another precious textile instead. Premade embellishments—paper or millinery flowers—tied on with ribbon make this set especially easy to assemble quickly. (Just steer clear of new silk flowers—they tend to lack the elegant appearance that these projects need.)

Together with their families,
Dan & Anne
joyously invite you to a cocktail party
to celebrate their engagement
Friday, the third of November
at eight in the evening

Traditional Wedding Tag

This design is so easy and pretty that you may want to use it for place cards as well as for gift tags. To create, mount floral paper onto illustration board, cut out a large tag shape, punch a hole at the end, thread ribbon through the hole, and tie on a few small flowers.

Traditional Wedding Invitation

This standard framed flat card has a few extra touches. I printed the invitation message onto light pink vellum and aged the edges of the frame with brown ink (see Aging Paper on page 17) before adhering the two layers together. Then I glued on velvet leaves and added strips of parchment paper with the couple's names.

Together with their families,
DAN & ANNE
joyously invite you to a cocktail party
to celebrate their engagement
Friday, the third of November
at eight in the evening

Traditional Wedding Card

For a truly sumptuous card, use a raised bouquet as a focal point. First, create a base card and age the edges with brown ink. Then cut a slit in the middle of the fold, thread a wide satin ribbon through the slit, and tie it at the front of the card. Hot-glue a bouquet of millinery flowers to the knot, tie a miniature card to the ribbon, and tie the ribbon into a bow. Write the couple's names and their wedding date inside the miniature card.

Wedding Cakes

Cakes are among my favorite images to use on celebration cards because they give a cardmaker so much room for invention. You can have as many layers as you want, make them as thick as you want, and use whatever colors and patterns tickle your fancy. And your embellishments can be as simple as strips of crimped paper or as elaborate as ribbon and silk flowers.

Wedding Cake Tag

I never worry about making the layers of my paper cake creations exactly perfect; to me, a little asymmetry only adds to the charm of a handmade tag. For this project, glue paper rectangles onto illustration board, cut out the cake shape, and embellish the cake as desired. I used pink rickrack trim for "frosting," green felt trim at the bottom, and crimped paper strips accented with tiny silk flowers.

Wedding Cake Card

Although the cake image for this card is wider and shorter than that of the Wedding Cake Tag, I created it in the same way, by adhering paper rectangles to illustration board, then cutting out the cake shape. To give the cake some dimension, I used foam dots to mount it to the base and applied a thick trim for the frosting.

Wedding Cake Invitation

Rather than a standard folded base card, this design makes use of two separate rectangles of cardstock tied together with ribbons along the left edge. Because my text, "A Wedding Shower," has three words, I chose to create three layers for my cake so that each word could appear on a separate line; spreading out the message prevented the card from becoming cluttered. To give the main image extra impact, I added a tall cake stand to the bottom and a bright red millinery flower to the top.

Wedding Dresses

Bridal showers, bachelorette parties, gifts for the bride—there are many occasions when you might need cards with an all-out feminine look. And while nothing gets as girly as miniature bridal gowns, a careful choice of background patterns can prevent charming from becoming cutesy. I felt that a mostly cream paper did the trick for my cards, but I encourage you to experiment and trust your own eyes.

Wedding Dress Flat Card

The wedding dresses for all the cards in this set are created in the same way: cut out the shape, gather a small piece of tulle with your fingers, and use fast-drying glue to adhere the gathered end of the fabric to the waist of the dress form. Cover the gathers with ribbon and embellish the gown as desired, then attach it to your base card. (The Dress pattern is available on page 140.) To make this particular flat card, simply use foam dots to apply a dress to a paper rectangle with scalloped edges, set an eyelet in the top of the card, and finish with a pink ribbon.

Wedding Dress Tag

When working with the designs in this set, remember to alter the dress shape as needed in order to enhance your design. Here, I cut the dress shorter to better complement the thin, vertical card. Placing the dress image on the right edge of the base gives this tag more dimension, while brown ink dabbed along the edge enriches the tag with a vintage feel.

Wedding Dress Card

This card looks more complicated than it is. First, cut a card base from heavyweight scrapbook paper (or paper mounted on cardstock), leaving about an inch extra on the right side to create a flap. Score and fold the base. Cover the front of the flap with a coordinating paper and trim the edge with scalloped scissors. Punch two holes in the flap, thread a decorative ribbon through them, and tie. Create a dress and use foam dots to apply it to the card.

Blue Florals

Inspiration for this set came from a Victorian paper doll and an antique floral wallpaper, but you can substitute scrapbook paper for the backgrounds, and either an image from vintage ephemera or a photo of the bride-to-be. To enhance the old-fashioned feel of your materials, brush brown ink along the edges of the cards and use ivory embellishments.

Bridal Showers

Blue Floral Wedding Card

Part of the fun of making a card like this is the opportunity it provides for finding inventive ways to use leftover scraps of your favorite materials. For my bridal card, I used a wisp of a feather as a headdress, created a skirt from a bit of ivory lace, then added a tiny flower, pearl beads, and crystal glitter.

Blue Floral Shower Invitation

The raised elements make this design seem more complex than it is, but once you've gathered your materials, it takes only about 15 minutes to make each card. To create the base, score and fold blue floral paper, and age its edges with brown ink (see Aging Paper on page 17). Next, embellish the paper doll and use foam dots to apply it to the card base. Add a banner trimmed with pinking shears, then cut a paper parasol in half and adhere it in place with fine-tipped glue. Note that if your paper doll isn't the right size for the card, you can enlarge or reduce it (as I did) when you copy it.

Blue Floral Wedding Tag

To create this project, I made a tag-shaped base using the blue floral papers and added the vintage image embellished with rhinestones and a lace veil. Sheer seam-binding ribbon, threaded through a hole in the top and then tied, finished the tag. If you need to make multiple tags quickly, consider shortcuts such as using premade base tags or minimizing the embellishments on the image.

Chic Wedding

Sophisticated, gender-neutral wedding designs are easy to achieve—just reach for geometrics in subtle colors and use clean, minimalistic layouts. To keep simple from appearing simplistic, pay special attention to details. For instance, to give the designs shown here a more formal feel, I sprayed adhesive and applied a layer of crystal glitter to the base card of each project before I added embellishments. (The images used for the charms are available on page 141.)

Chic Wedding Card

Because this design takes a little more time to make than the Chic Wedding Tag, I recommend it for bridal shower or rehearsal dinner invitations—occasions that typically call for fewer cards. To create the base, mount two coordinated papers onto the front of a top-folded piece of cardstock. Spray with adhesive and sprinkle with crystal glitter. When the glue is dry, apply a silky ribbon across the seam between the papers and attach an embellished, gold-edged charm by tying gold cord around the entire cover of the card.

Square Chic Wedding Card

An understated design with a simple color scheme doesn't need a large, flashy embellishment to have an eye-catching focal point. With pale papers, a small gold-edged charm on a gold cord can be the right accent.

Chic Wedding Tag

Once you've gathered your materials, this tag takes about five minutes to make, which is great news if you need to make multiples. First, color copy the cupcake image at a size appropriate to your charm. Cut out the image and adhere it to the center of the charm. Next, punch a large oval from one heavyweight paper and a tag shape from another, punch small holes in the top of each one, and use gold cord to tie them together with a charm. Attach the tag to a small white bag that holds a wedding favor or an attendant's gift.

Bridal Bouquet

With minimal embellishments, this set is easy to make quickly. Make sure, however, that your background papers coordinate well with the main image; the time-saving simplicity of this card leaves you less room than a more elaborate project might to adjust the design with more elements. Color copy the Bouquet image (available on page 141), mount it on illustration board, and, if you wish, add touches of crystal glitter before applying it to the background.

Bridal Bouquet Invitation

The base of this card is really a color copy of the original. First, create a master of a framed flat card, with the invitation message inside the window (see Color Copy Messages on page 14). Next, make as many color copies of the master and the Bouquet Image as needed. Mount the copies onto illustration board, cut them out, and adhere a bouquet to the top of each base card.

Bridal Bouquet Tag

To create this tag, either punch or cut out a large circle from pink cardstock and a smaller circle from aqua cardstock. Punch small holes around the edge of the larger circle to create a lacelike effect. Place the bouquet image over the smaller circle and punch two holes on either side of the bouquet's flower stems. Thread a ribbon or cord through the holes and secure the image to the smaller circle by tying the ends into a bow. Use foam tape to apply the smaller circle to the larger one. Thread a ribbon or cord through one of the "lace" holes to attach the tag to a gift.

Bridal Bouquet Card

When working with pastels, it can be tricky to balance a soft, romantic mood with well-defined elements. For this card, and for the Easy Wedding Invitation, I wanted a sharper effect than that of the Soft Florals series (see pages 36 and 37), so I chose a paper with floral stripes. The touches of yellow and red in the bouquet image—which are not mirrored in the background—enhance its presence on the card.

To:

From:

Wedding Wishes

Thank You

Spring Wedding

Gentle pastels, translucent vellum, and seam-binding ribbon give these designs their bridal feel. For an authentic, old-time look, I color copied authentic, old-time wallpaper to use on three of the four projects, pairing it with a striped scrapbook paper for a refreshing combination.

Spring Wedding Tag

What do spring showers bring? Gifts for the bride and groom, naturally! Pretty up a present or a place setting with an umbrella-shaped tag cut from floral paper, embellished with rickrack, and finished with a pipe-cleaner handle. (The Umbrella pattern is available on page 141.)

Spring Wedding Card

There's nothing like layering to give a card a luxurious appearance—unless it's layering layers! Here, a simple base card gets a border of crimped, scalloped paper that's adhered to the inside edge of the cover. For the center, strips of tulle and crimped paper are held in place by a sheer, rhinestone-bejeweled ribbon wrapped around the entire cover. Because too much is never enough for a card like this, the embellishment is layered, too: a small paper heart with the words "Wedding Wishes" is set onto a larger heart bordered with German mirror flake and topped with a paper flower. The last detail is an angel image adhered to the back of a flat-backed marble and hot-glued to the center of the flower.

Spring Wedding Thank-You Card

The presentation of a heart-shaped miniature tag makes this card unusual. After tying a ribbon around the fold, I glued a heart punched from vellum and bordered with rhinestones to the ends of the ribbon. If you don't trust your handwriting or have many cards to make, purchase a rubber stamp of the words "Thank You" in script and customize the size of the heart to hold the text.

Spring Wedding Invitation

A simple invitation printed on vellum becomes a rich confection when it's slipped into a handmade embellished band. Adhere layers of paper, wrap a ribbon around it, and complete the card with punched-out hearts, a fabric flower, and a miniature tag.

Gift Giving

When you make your own cards, you need never be at a loss for gifts or imaginative new ways to present them. I often start with an unusual container picked up inexpensively at a flea market and then design a set of cards to go with it. Since everyone needs to send a card now and then, such gifts are practical as well as fun. And by making a container part of the gift, you make it easier for the recipient to keep the cards neat and organized until they're ready to use them.

Made In Dominican Republic.

Writing Desks

Once upon a time, every woman had her own writing desk fitted out with everything that she needed to keep up with her correspondence. If you need a gift for someone who still prefers handwriting letters to sending e-mail, create a new version of the writing desk with one of these first two projects.

Made In Dominican Republic.

Cigar Box Writing Desk

Here's the perfect gift for the friend who appreciates handmade cards but doesn't have the time to create them herself. Start by embellishing a cigar box (often free or very inexpensive at cigar shops) then fill it with your own cards, tags, and envelopes. If there's room, slip in a pen or two and packet of stamps. If left smooth, the top of the box can make a nice writing surface.

Clipboard Writing Desk

Designed to provide both a writing surface and stationery supplies in one neat package, this project is an ideal gift for a bed-bound friend. To create the project, first decoupage an ordinary clipboard with pretty papers, taking care to keep the main writing surface smooth. Then string an elastic ribbon across the bottom and tuck in glassine envelopes filled with stamps and mailing labels. Add a few of your own handmade cards and tags, and tie on a pen or pencil; your friend will have all she needs to keep in touch the old-fashioned way.

Embellished Gift Bag

Show off your handmade cards by presenting them in a windowed gift bag. Begin with a gift bag that complements the style of your cards. Cut a rectangular window into one side of the bag and use double-sided tape to adhere an acetate panel across the hole. Embellish the bag as desired. (I used hot glue to adhere pompoms and a bow.)

Embellished Tags

A collection of pretty tags found at a craft store becomes a great gift when you trim the bottom edges with scalloped scissors and add ribbons to the tops. Slip the tags into a clear glass tied with hat netting (available in fabric stores), and embellish the glass with a fabric leaf and some flowers.

New Parent Gift Basket

New parents have endless folks to thank, from kind friends and neighbors to especially helpful medical personnel. Make it easier for them to express their appreciation with a basket of stylish handmade cards. To be extra nice, put postage stamps on the envelopes and include a stuffed animal.

Embellished Flowerpot

For the gardener in your life, create a flower-themed gift. Start by creating a set of pocket cards with different packets of seeds, label a planting marker with the sentiment "Planting Seeds of Friendship," and tuck them into a clay pot decorated with ribbon, paper strips, and a tag. For the final touch, turn an ordinary pen into a flower by holding the stem of a fabric flower to the barrel of a pen and wrapping green florist's tape around them.

Teapot Gift Basket

One of the great advantages to making your own cards is that you can customize their sizes and designs to suit any nifty container. A flea market teapot—bought for a song because it was missing its lid—became a gift basket when I filled it with a set of teacup cards specially designed to match its style.

Vintage Metal Basket

Fans of the vintage look will appreciate handmade stationery presented in a gracefully aged container such as this metal basket. Taking my cue from the floral design on the front of the basket, I turned a pen into a flower (see the Embellished Flowerpot project on page 127), added a gift tag, and, using more florist's tape, attached a flower to the handle of the basket. The result is a memorable presentation for a set of handmade cards.

Angel Art

This section contains illustrations and patterns to help you re-create many of the projects in this book. As the name Angel Art implies, this artwork is my gift to you. Like the projects in this book, you may duplicate and use these images for personal projects, provided that you do not sell them. Keep in mind that you can reduce or enlarge images using a color copier to suit your project.

Aqua Dress Pattern

Pink Dress Pattern

Dress and Crown

Bear and Cupcake

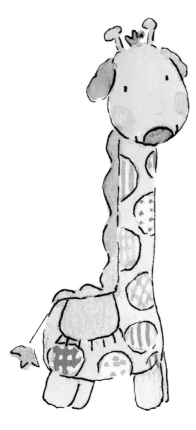

Giraffe

Elephant

Cars and Truck

Fire Truck

Train

Fairy Godbunny

Contemporary Lamb

Bear in Floral Carriage

Bear in Green Carriage

Soft Floral Cake

Soft Floral Bouquet

Duckling

Bear with Heart

Gingham Bunny

Baby Shower

Umbrella
Carriage

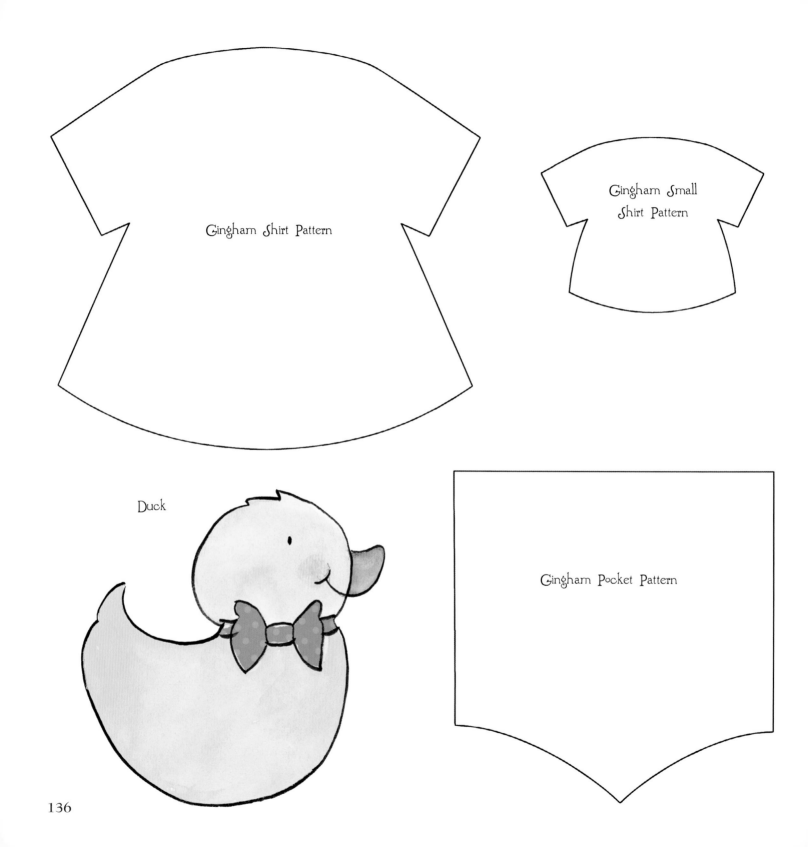

Gingham Shirt Pattern

Gingham Small
Shirt Pattern

Duck

Gingham Pocket Pattern

136

Teapot Pattern

Dreidel Pattern
(Card)

Dreidel Pattern (Tag)

Heart Pattern

Teacup Pattern

Basic Santa

Heart Mice

Stocking Pattern

Flower Mice

138

Telephone Pattern

It's been tooooooooo long

I miss you

Dachshund

Pink Felt Dress Pattern

Skirt and Blouse Pattern

Blue Felt Dress
Pattern

Blue Felt Sweater
Pattern

Cocktail Glass

Pink Drink

Wedding Dress Pattern

Tall Cake Charm   Cake Charm   Cupcake Charm

Bridal Bouquet

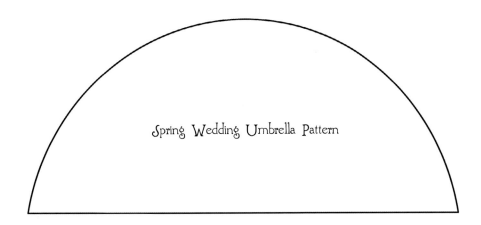

Spring Wedding Umbrella Pattern

Credits

Writer/Editor: Jennifer Gibbs

Copyeditor: Chris Rich

Book Designer: Rose Sheifer

Photographers: Ryne Hazen and Steve Mann

Stylists: Jo Packham and Chris Bryant

Cover and Section Openers: Heidi VanWinkle

Some of the projects in this book contain images from the following collections by Dover Publications:

Adventures of Dolly Dingle Paper Dolls
by Grace G. Drayton, 38–39

Old–Time Vignettes in Full Color
by Carol Belanger Grafton, 32–33. 46–47, and 110–111

Old–Time Children Vignettes in Full Color
by Carol Belanger Grafton, 50–51

Old–Fashioned Food and Drink Stickers
by Carol Belanger Grafton, 38

Old–Time Romantic Vignettes in Full Color
by Carol Belanger Grafton, 88–89

Special thanks to my friend Julia Minasian for allowing me to share her handmade card on page 8.

Metric Conversion Chart

INCHES	METRIC (MM/CM)	INCHES	METRIC (MM/CM)	INCHES	METRIC (MM/CM)	INCHES	METRIC (MM/CM)	INCHES	METRIC (MM/CM)	INCHES	METRIC (MM/CM)
$1/4$	6 mm	1	2.5 cm	$8^{1}/_{2}$	21.6 cm	16	40.6 cm	$23^{1}/_{2}$	59.7 cm	31	78.7 cm
$1/8$	3 mm	$1^{1}/_{2}$	3.8 cm	9	22.9 cm	$16^{1}/_{2}$	41.9 cm	24	61 cm	$31^{1}/_{2}$	80 cm
$3/16$	5 mm	2	5 cm	$9^{1}/_{2}$	24.1 cm	17	43.2 cm	$24^{1}/_{2}$	62.2 cm	32	81.3 cm
$1/4$	6 mm	$2^{1}/_{2}$	6.4 cm	10	25.4 cm	$17^{1}/_{2}$	44.5 cm	25	63.5 cm	$32^{1}/_{2}$	82.6 cm
$5/16$	8 mm	3	7.6 cm	$10^{1}/_{2}$	26.7 cm	18	45.7 cm	$25^{1}/_{2}$	64.8 cm	33	83.8 cm
$3/8$	9.5 mm	$3^{1}/_{2}$	8.9 cm	11	27.9 cm	$18^{1}/_{2}$	47 cm	26	66 cm	$33^{1}/_{2}$	85 cm
$7/16$	1.1 cm	4	10.2 cm	$11^{1}/_{2}$	29.2 cm	19	48.3 cm	$26^{1}/_{2}$	67.3 cm	34	86.4 cm
$1/2$	1.3 cm	$4^{1}/_{2}$	11.4 cm	12	30.5 cm	$19^{1}/_{2}$	49.5 cm	27	68.6 cm	$34^{1}/_{2}$	87.6 cm
$9/16$	1.4 cm	5	12.7 cm	$12^{1}/_{2}$	31.8 cm	20	50.8 cm	$27^{1}/_{2}$	69.9 cm	35	88.9 cm
$5/8$	1.6 cm	$5^{1}/_{2}$	14 cm	13	33 cm	$20^{1}/_{2}$	52 cm	28	71.1 cm	$35^{1}/_{2}$	90.2 cm
$11/16$	1.7 cm	6	15.2 cm	$13^{1}/_{2}$	34.3 cm	21	53.3	$28^{1}/_{2}$	72.4 cm	36	91.4 cm
$3/4$	1.9 cm	$6^{1}/_{2}$	16.5 cm	14	35.6 cm	$21^{1}/_{2}$	54.6	29	73.7 cm	$36^{1}/_{2}$	92.7 cm
$13/16$	2.1 cm	7	17.8 cm	$14^{1}/_{2}$	36.8 cm	22	55 cm	$29^{1}/_{2}$	74.9 cm	37	94.0 cm
$7/8$	2.2 cm	$7^{1}/_{2}$	19 cm	15	38.1 cm	$22^{1}/_{2}$	57.2 cm	30	76.2 cm	$37^{1}/_{2}$	95.3 cm
$15/16$	2.4 cm	8	20.3 cm	$15^{1}/_{2}$	39.4 cm	23	58.4 cm	$30^{1}/_{2}$	77.5 cm	38	96.5 cm

Index